DIST*UN*ACTED

Capture Your Purpose
Rediscover Your Joy

STUDY GUIDE | FIVE SESSIONS

BOB GOFF

Harper*Christian*
Resources

Undistracted Study Guide
© 2022 by Bob Goff

Requests for information should be addressed to:
HarperChristian Resources, 3900 Sparks Dr. SE, Grand Rapids, Michigan 49546

ISBN 978-0-310-14845-6 (softcover)
ISBN 978-0-310-14846-3 (ebook)

HarperChristian Resources titles may be purchased in bulk for church, business, fundraising, or ministry use. For information, please e-mail ResourceSpecialist@ChurchSource.com.

Published in association with Alive Literary Agency, www.aliveliterary.com.

First Printing February 2022 / Printed in the United States of America

CONTENTS

INTRODUCTION

Distractions. Like flies buzzing around a picnic, they seem inevitable to the human experience. You can barely begin your day without distractions grabbing your attention. Unexpected circumstances divert your focus and send you down unfamiliar detours. Urgent problems consume the energy you had planned to expend on fulfilling goals. Other people derail the tasks you're determined to complete. Relationships get complicated and require resources that you hadn't anticipated expending. You can get so distracted sometimes that you lose sight of why you're doing what you're doing and who you're doing it for.

Even worse, distractions can pull you away from spending time with God, from those you love, and from what you long to contribute to the world. As your attention drifts, you can get stuck in the past, worry about the present, and get distracted by the future instead of realizing the opportunities you have right now and right where you are. Distractions can cause you to compare yourself to others and try to act like somebody else instead of the unique person that God created you to be. They can even compel you to chase after goals that offer hollow satisfaction . . . and then you wonder why you're so exhausted and stressed all the time.

The purpose of this study is to help you identify these kinds of distractions, eliminate them, recharge and refocus your efforts, and then start living a less-distracted and more joy-filled life. It is to help you say *no* to the things that are taking you away from your goals so you can say *yes* to the greater opportunities that God wants to place in your life. This is something you have permission to do! When driving on the highway, no one asks for permission to stay on the road—and you don't need permission to live a more fulfilling life either. You can decide right now to live the rich, meaningful, and beautiful life that God has already given you.

Regardless of your age or stage of life, now is the perfect time to drill down and get clear on what you are actually aiming for in your life. It is time to discover how to get undistracted in your *attitude,* in your *service,* in your *relationships,* in your *faith,* and in your *purpose.* It is time to ask what those purposeful things are in your life that will go the distance—traits like faith, hope, joy, purpose, and love. These are the things Jesus said would outlast everything else. Once you have identified them in your life, then it's time to get busy implementing them. And there's no better place for this kind of work than the group you're in!

HOW TO USE
THIS GUIDE

The *Undistracted* video study is designed to be experienced in a group setting (such as a Bible study, Sunday school class, or small group gathering) and also as an individual study. Each session begins with a welcome section, two questions to get you thinking about the topic, and a brief reading from the Bible. You will then watch a video with Bob Goff, which can be accessed via the streaming code found on the inside front cover.

If you are doing this study with a group, you will then engage in some directed discussion and close with a time of personal reflection and prayer. Each person in the group should have his or her own copy of this study guide, and you are also encouraged to have a copy of the *Undistracted* book, as reading it alongside the curriculum will provide you with deeper insights. (See the "For Next Week" section at the end of each between-studies section for the chapters in the book that correspond to material you are discussing.)

To get the most out of your group experience, keep the following points in mind. First, the real growth in this study will happen during your small-group time. This is where you will process the content of the teaching for the week, ask questions, and learn from others as you hear what God is doing in their lives. For this reason, it is important for you to be fully committed to the group and attend each session so you can build trust and rapport with the other members. If you choose to only go through the motions, or if you refrain from participating, there is a lesser chance you will find what you're looking for during this study.

Second, remember that the goal of your small group is to serve as a place where people can share, learn about God, and build intimacy and friendship. For this reason, seek to make your group a safe place. This means being honest about your thoughts and feelings and listening carefully to everyone else's opinion. (If you are a group leader, there are additional instructions and resources in the back of the book for leading a productive discussion group.)

Third, resist the temptation to fix a problem someone might be having or to correct his or her theology, as that's not the purpose of your small-group time. Also, keep everything your group shares confidential. This will foster a rewarding sense of community in your group and create a place where people can heal, be challenged, and grow spiritually.

Following your group time, reflect on the material you've covered by engaging in any or all of the between-sessions activities. For each session, you may wish to complete the personal study all in one sitting or spread it out over five days. Note that if you are unable to finish (or even start) your between-sessions personal study, you can still attend the group study video session. You are wanted and welcome even if you don't have your "homework" done.

Keep in mind that the videos, discussion questions, and activities are simply meant to kick-start your imagination so you are open to what God wants you to hear and how he wants you to apply it. As you go through this study, listen to what he is saying and consider your own journey in light of the distractions that you are facing in your life.

Sound good? Then let's get started!

UNDISTRACTED IN OUR ATTITUDE

Love the Lord your God with all your heart and
with all your soul and with all your mind.

MATTHEW 22:37

WELCOME

How many decisions do you suppose you make in an average day? A half-dozen? Twenty? Fifty? One hundred? Studies have shown that on average, most adults make around 35,000 decisions each and every day. Now, some of these decisions are minor concerns, like whether to have Raisin Bran or Pop-Tarts, which blouse or shirt to wear, and whether to drive or take the bus. But some are weightier decisions: *Should you apply for that new position? Have the conversation with your boss? Take the next step in your relationship? Ask your kids some hard questions?*

Dealing with all these choices can leave you feeling exhausted, afraid, anxious, uncertain, confused, angry, worried . . . and a host of other emotions. Based on sheer volume, all these decisions can also leave you feeling incredibly distracted. The trivial and mundane decisions can blur into the more significant choices you make. It requires time, reflection, prayer, and due diligence to take giant steps in life. But when bombarded with thousands of other seemingly urgent demands, it can be hard to focus your attention on how to align your decisions and actions with your values and convictions.

Your decisions aren't the only variable influencing your attitude, but they definitely contribute to how you spend most of your time, focus your attention, and pursue various activities. Your decisions are also influenced by the assumptions you've made and accepted as truth and by the stories you have told yourself. You probably know that not all stories and assumptions should be shaping the choices you make, but you may have a blind spot in seeing how certain ones are holding you back, keeping you distracted, and blurring your focus.

It's been said that decisions shape who you are. But what if instead "who you are" shapes the decisions you make? What if your identity, purpose, and faith in God guided the way you prioritized the decisions you make? If you want to be undistracted in your attitude, it's time to take an honest look at your decisions and what's consuming your time and attention.

SHARE

It you or any of your group members are just getting to know one another, take a few minutes to introduce yourselves. Then, to get things started, discuss one of the following questions:

- What is something you consider to be a big distraction in your life right now?

— *or* —

- In the course of an average day, how often does your mind wander?

READ

Invite someone to read aloud the following passage. Listen for fresh insights as you hear the verses being read and then discuss the questions that follow.

> Praise be to the God and Father of our Lord Jesus Christ, the Father of compassion and the God of all comfort, who comforts us in all our troubles, so that we can comfort those in any trouble with the comfort we ourselves receive from God. For just as we share abundantly in the sufferings of Christ, so also our comfort abounds through Christ. If we are distressed, it is for your comfort and salvation; if we are comforted, it is for your comfort, which produces in you patient endurance of the same sufferings we suffer. And our hope for you is firm, because we know that just as you share in our sufferings, so also you share in our comfort.
>
> *2 Corinthians 1:3–7*

How have you experienced the comfort of God in times of trouble?

When has "patient endurance" in sufferings helped you comfort and console other people who were suffering? What did you have to offer them because of what you had experienced?

WATCH

Play the video segment for session one (use the streaming video access provided on the inside front cover). As you watch, use the following outline to record any thoughts or concepts that stand out to you.

You want to have an awesome attitude? Be where your feet are. Be self-aware. Be situationally aware. Be emotionally aware. Be spiritually aware.

Jesus talked about loving God with your heart and your soul and your mind (see Matthew 22:37). He talked about loving your neighbors like yourself (see Mark 12:31). He talked about loving widows and orphans and doing things for people that were hurting (see Matthew 25:35–36).

Pilots follow a **GUMPS** checklist for flying that can also help us keep our focus:

Gas: What is fueling your ambitions and joy?

Undercarriage: Are you prepared for what is ahead?

Mixture: How are you applying your energy?

Propeller: Are you moving forward or just spinning in place?

Seat Belts: What is the basis for your security?

As you take off into this time, think about the following questions: *What am I doing? Why am I doing it?* **What's distracting me from my purpose?**

Find out the **stories that you've made** about your life. Maybe some of the stories are about how you perceive yourself—*I just can't be that person, I need to be quiet,* or *I need to be gregarious and loud and silly.* Figure out the stories that you have made up about yourself along the way.

Distraction comes at a high cost. Think about it . . . what is it costing you to be distracted by an iPhone, old relationships that aren't squared away, and new ones that are crazy? It's costing us a ton.

The Bible says that God comforts us in our failures and times of sadness so that we can comfort other people with the comfort we got from him (see 2 Corinthians 1:3–4). Don't be taken offline by setbacks. You can **turn a distraction in your past into a bright future.**

When you are undistracted in your attitude, your joy and peace and willingness to serve becomes contagious. When you are "on tone," everybody else
will be on tone as well.

DISCUSS

As you consider what you just watched, use the following
questions to discuss these ideas, their basis in Scripture, and
their application in your life with your group members.

1. What does it mean to you to "be where your feet are"? What are some
   ways you try to remain present each day?

2. What are the biggest distractions in your life right now? How would you
   describe or characterize them?

3. Do you agree that your primary focus should be on loving God completely,
   loving others as yourself, and serving those in need? Why or why not?

4. What false stories have you been able to identify so far in your life? What impact have those false stories had on your identity and purpose?

5. Why is it so challenging to shift the focus from your own pain in the midst of trials to those who might be suffering as well? When have you experienced giving comfort to others based on storms that you've already encountered?

6. When has your attitude been positively affected by someone else's positivity, compassion, and ability to be present to you and your needs? When have you been able to pass this kind of attitude on to someone else?

LEARN

As you reflect on this week's teaching and the group discussion, consider how you can remain open to new ways of eliminating distractions and keeping your focus on what matters most. To facilitate this process, at the end of each session you will find an exercise designed to help you apply the teaching so you can become undistracted and more present in your life. This practice will also be a way to help others in your group as you learn and grow together.

In this first session, you've started the process of exploring what it means to recognize distractions in your life and how you can refocus your *attitude*. Get a sheet of paper and write GUMPS as a vertical column on the left side of the page. Take a few minutes and fill in your assessment of this flight checklist as it applies to where you are in life. Use your video teaching notes to prompt your assessment for each category: Gas, Undercarriage, Mixture, Propeller, Seat Belts. You might also list specific distractions you're aware of within each category. Keep this checklist handy so you can review it later during times of personal study.

PRAY

Conclude your session by sharing any requests you would like the group to lift up in prayer. Thank God for bringing you together for this study so you can help and encourage one another as you seek to recognize and overcome the distractions. Ask God to give you clarity, wisdom, and discernment as you proceed. Trust that he will give you eyes to see and ears to hear the truth of how, when, and where to focus your time, attention, energy, and resources.

PERSONAL STUDY

Reflect on everything you've covered in session one of *Undistracted* by engaging in any or all of the between-sessions activities that follow. Keep in mind this part of the study is not about doing homework or following a set of rules. These activities are simply designed to maximize opportunities to bring your dreams to life. First, you will **Reflect** on a passage from Scripture related to the main points of your last group session. Next, you will **Refocus** on the priorities of your life as you identify and eliminate distractions you're facing. Finally, you will **Recharge** by applying what you've been learning in simple and practical ways. For this first personal study, you will find it helpful to have read chapters 5, 7, 10, and 15 in *Undistracted*. At the start of the next session, you will have a few minutes to share any insights you learned with the group.

REFLECT

As you begin identifying the distractions that pull you away from your focus, it is helpful to hit pause at times and reflect on where you are in your life right now. The book of Psalms can be helpful in this respect because it is filled with the experiences of individuals who took such moments to stop and reflect on their situation, purpose, and what God was doing in their lives. Keep this goal in mind as you read the passage below and answer the questions that follow.

> You have searched me, LORD,
>   and you know me.
> You know when I sit and when I rise;
>   you perceive my thoughts from afar.
> You discern my going out and my lying down;
>   you are familiar with all my ways.
> Before a word is on my tongue
>   you, LORD, know it completely.
> You hem me in behind and before,
>   and you lay your hand upon me.
> Such knowledge is too wonderful for me,
>   too lofty for me to attain. . . .
> For you created my inmost being;
>   you knit me together in my mother's womb.
> I praise you because I am fearfully and
> wonderfully made;
>   your works are wonderful,
>   I know that full well.

Psalm 139:1–6, 13–14

How do you feel as you consider that God, the one who created you, knows you better than you know yourself? How can being reminded of this truth help you eliminate distractions?

Considering that God knows you intimately, why is it important to ask him to search your heart? What is he wanting to reveal to you about what's in your heart right now?

What does it mean to you to be "fearfully and wonderfully made"? How does this truth anchor you to the unique purpose for which God created you?

Reread the passage and ask God to give you wisdom on how to overcome obstacles that are impacting your attitude. Thank him for how he is helping you to move forward.

REFOCUS

It's tempting to fall into the trap of believing that we will be happy *someday*. We tell ourselves, "I'll be happy *someday* when I finish my degree . . . get the right job . . . meet the right person . . . have kids . . . or when the kids finally move out." All too often, we consider happiness to be something *out there* that we need to attain. But such an attitude only serves to keep us looking ahead to the future instead of enjoying where we are in the present and what you have right now. The apostle Paul knew how easy it is to make contentment conditional in this way, but he had also learned the secret of eliminating this distraction-trap. Read through his words on this subject below and then answer the questions that follow.

> Rejoice in the Lord always. I will say it again: Rejoice! Let your gentleness be evident to all. The Lord is near. Do not be anxious about anything, but in every situation, by prayer and petition, with thanksgiving, present your requests to God. And the peace of God, which transcends all understanding, will guard your hearts and your minds in Christ Jesus. . . .
>
> I rejoiced greatly in the Lord that at last you renewed your concern for me. Indeed, you were concerned, but you had no opportunity to show it. I am not saying this because I am in need, for I have learned to be content whatever the circumstances. I know what it is to be in need, and I know what it is to have plenty. I have learned the secret of being content in any and every situation,

whether well fed or hungry, whether living in plenty or in
want. I can do all this through him who gives me strength.

Philippians 4:4–7, 10–13

Paul states he had "learned to be content whatever the
circumstances." This includes being content in the *present*.
Despite the trials he endured—angry mobs, beatings, ship-
wrecks, snakebites, and more (see 2 Corinthians 11:24–29)—
he was able to find contentment. The same can be true for
you if you rely on the same spiritual power source. You can
declare, "I *will* be content and I *will* be present" without
waiting on any future goals, accomplishments, or milestones
to be attained. While you can never completely control your
circumstances or anticipate all the setbacks you will face,
you can ask God to help you spot any distractions that are
obscuring your view of what he's already doing and where
he wants to take you next.

When have you chosen to rejoice in the Lord right where you were rather than
make your joy conditional on future events? What were the consequences
of making such a choice?

According to Paul, what is the secret of overcoming anxiety? How could you apply his solution to any anxiety that is currently having a negative impact on your attitude?

When you consider what you face most days, what distracts you most from experiencing the kind of contentment and "peace which transcends all understanding" that Paul describes?

What are three things you can thank God for providing right now? How does focusing on gratitude and counting your blessings help to eliminate distractions in your attitude?

RECHARGE

If you want to live a more undistracted life, you will need to get honest with yourself and acknowledge the distractions that you accept and accommodate. The blanket term "busyness" is one of the greatest culprits for distracting your focus and stealing your joy. So, if you want to see change in your life, take a realistic look at where you are right now and how you spend your time on most days. On a separate sheet of paper, draw a large circle—or, better yet, use a paper plate if you have one. Think of this circle (or plate) as the twenty-four hours you have to spend each day. Now think about how many hours you spend doing the following activities, blocking out or shading that amount of your twenty-four-hour circle. Again, choose an average day filled with most of the responsibilities, relationships, and realities you usually encounter.

- Sleeping
- Working (both on-site and at-home)
- Exercising / self-care (working out, walking, stretching, playing sports)
- Praying / Bible study / time with God
- Volunteering / serving
- Connecting with family (talking, listening, sharing activities, caring)
- Connecting with friends and neighbors (talking, listening, helping, serving)
- Other (anything else you do most days not included above)

After you've shaded or blocked out all of the hours in your circle, take a look at what is really consuming your time. Other than sleep, what takes up most of your time each day? How important is this activity to you?

Are what and who you care about most accurately depicted in your circle? How do you feel about these results?

What activities that you value are not being practiced regularly? What is lacking most in how you spend your hours each day?

If you showed your circle (and your answers to these questions) to a family member, close friend, or spouse, would they verify its accuracy? In other words, are you seeing clearly when it comes to how you're actually spending your time? Why or why not?

For Next Week: Write down any insights or questions you want to discuss at the next group meeting. In preparation for next week, read chapters 3, 8, and 13 in *Undistracted*.

UNDISTRACTED IN OUR SERVICE

Keep on loving one another as brothers and sisters. Do not forget to show hospitality to strangers, for by so doing some people have shown hospitality to angels without knowing it.

HEBREWS 13:1-2

WELCOME

All too often, events in life don't turn out the way that you had hoped or expected. A text severs a decade-long business partnership. Someone else gets the last spot in the new training program. The flight gets cancelled. The car breaks down on the way to the airport. The hurricane hits. The resources dry up. The offer gets rejected.

These last-minute curveballs can be downright confusing, especially when you're doing what you think you are supposed to be doing. But that's just it . . . what if what you think you're supposed to be doing isn't really the point? What if the point is to make the most of *wherever* you are *whenever* you're there? Basically, to be giving and caring and serving those around you regardless of what you thought, hoped, expected, or planned?

The reality is that distractions will *always* pull you away from plans, schedules, goals . . . and especially volunteer opportunities. But just as God calls you to follow Christ every day and not just on Sundays or when you are attending church, so serving others requires a constant focus that is undistracted by all the unexpected twists and turns that you will encounter. You don't have to wait until the conditions are just right or until you think you're ready to serve. You don't have to go overseas on a missions trip. You can help people right where you are.

You don't have to be the smartest, richest, most talented, or most experienced person to serve the needs of those around you. Your motives don't even have to be pure! You simply have to be *available*. When you look at the stories of Jesus told in the Bible, you find that even though he was often tired (if not exhausted), not to mention frustrated by those plotting against him, he was always *available* to help those in need.

Following Jesus means following his example. As we will discuss in this session, this means being undistracted in your service . . . to move past distractions, see the needs around you, and meet them as best you can. After all, if we say we love God but don't love and serve the people he made—and this includes *all* people, even the strange and odd and ones slightly different from us—then we have a heart condition that we need to address.

SHARE

If you or any of your group members are just getting to know one another, take a few minutes to introduce yourselves and share any insights you have from last week's personal study. Then, to get things started, discuss one of the following questions:

- How do you usually react when an unexpected disruption derails your plans?

— *or* —

- Do you like to plan each day's activities out well ahead of time? Or do you like to improvise and be more spontaneous based on your mood?

READ

Invite someone to read aloud the following passage. Listen for fresh insights as you hear the verses being read and then discuss the questions that follow.

On one occasion an expert in the law stood up to test Jesus. "Teacher," he asked, "what must I do to inherit eternal life?"

"What is written in the Law?" he replied. "How do you read it?"

He answered, "'Love the Lord your God with all your heart and with all your soul and with all your strength and with all your mind'; and, 'Love your neighbor as yourself.'"

"You have answered correctly," Jesus replied. "Do this and you will live."

But he wanted to justify himself, so he asked Jesus, "And who is my neighbor?"

In reply Jesus said: "A man was going down from Jerusalem to Jericho, when he was attacked by robbers. They stripped him of his clothes, beat him and went away, leaving him half dead. A priest happened to be going down the same road, and when he saw the man, he passed by on the other side. So too, a Levite, when he came to the place and saw him, passed by on the other side. But a Samaritan, as he traveled, came where the man was; and when he saw him, he took pity on him. He went to him and bandaged his wounds, pouring on oil and wine. Then he put the man on his own donkey, brought him to an inn and took care of him. The next day he took out two denarii and gave them to the innkeeper. 'Look after him,' he said, 'and when I return, I will reimburse you for any extra expense you may have.'

"Which of these three do you think was a neighbor to the man who fell into the hands of robbers?"

The expert in the law replied, "The one who had mercy on him."

Jesus told him, "Go and do likewise."

Luke 10:25–37

Why do you think that Jesus answered the law expert's question—"who is my neighbor?"—with this story? What answer does the example of the Samaritan provide?

What might have distracted the priest and the Levite and kept them from helping the traveler? What is significant in the fact that the Samaritan stopped while the other two did not?

WATCH

Play the video segment for session two (use the streaming video access provided on the inside front cover). As you watch, use the following outline to record any thoughts or concepts that stand out to you.

What if God wants to surprise you? What if he wants to just surprise you with the relationships and the things that he has already put adjacent to you? You won't see them if you're distracted!

God didn't invite you to a business trip. He invited you on an *adventure*. And he has brought plenty of people along—some kind-of-odd ones and some really fun ones.

God wants us to have our heart start beating the way his heart is beating. His heart beats for the people who are hurting and lonely and isolated and afraid. **We can bring availability.**

Don't get head-faked when you encounter setbacks and don't get the things you really want. **Don't get distracted . . . get busy.** Start working on the next thing.

Would you reset your heart? What would you be willing to do to have your heart beat the way that Jesus' heart beats? The way that his heart beats for the poor, the disadvantaged, the lonely, the isolated? Could you get so available to people that you would actually stop your heart to start it again?

Get a new heartbeat. You can't be available to everybody all the time, but you can be available to somebody some of the time. Find that new rhythm and you will find yourself leaning into opportunities.

What can you launch in your world? What can you launch in the world of other people? It could be just one kind word from you. The *right* word from you.

Anticipate there will be great forward strides as well as the occasional setbacks. Don't get distracted when the setbacks come, and don't get distracted by your successes. Keep your eyes fixed on Jesus.

DISCUSS

As you consider what you just watched, use the following questions to discuss these ideas, their basis in Scripture, and their application in your life with your group members.

1. Can you think of ways that you're currently adjacent to places where God might want you to serve? What has prevented you from serving there so far?

2. How do you usually respond when your plans are disrupted? How do you *wish* you would respond?

3. When have you experienced what first appeared to be a disappointment only to see God turn it into an opportunity to serve others?

4. What does it look like for your heart to beat like God's heart beats? When have you experienced this kind of closeness that produced compassion for others?

5. How would you define *availability* when it comes to serving others? When was the last time you were available to meet the need of someone you encountered unexpectedly?

6. When it comes to service, how can successes distract you just as much as your setbacks?

LEARN

Pair up with another person in your group and briefly discuss how you are progressing in the main points covered in this session. Share with one another the distractions that prevent you from being available to serve those around you more frequently. Brainstorm how you can overcome those distractions and give of your time, attention, and energy more consistently. Come up with one specific strategy to help each other overcome distractions and concentrate more on serving. Use the following to guide your conversation:

FOR YOUR PARTNER

Daily distractions that prevent you from serving:

Strategies for overcoming these distractions:

Ways you can be more available for service:

FOR YOU

Daily distractions that prevent you from serving:

Strategies for overcoming these distractions:

Ways you can be more available for service:

After sharing your ideas, commit to praying for your partner and ask him or her to do the same for you. If you're willing, exchange contact information so you can check in at least once between this meeting and the group's next session.

PRAY

Return to the group and share any prayer requests. Don't be shy about expressing needs in your own life! Take a few minutes to pray together and thank God for all you are discovering about what it means to be undistracted and serve those around you. Ask him to give each of you eyes to see and ears to hear the needs of others and a heart that's always available.

PERSONAL STUDY

Take some time to reflect on the material you've covered this week by engaging in any or all of the following between-sessions activities. Remember, these exercises are not intended to be homework or another obligation in your busy week but are simply provided to help you process what you've been thinking and feeling since your last group time. At the start of the next session, you will have a few minutes to share any insights you learned.

REFLECT

When you think about serving others, you might picture some of the big ways that you can actively meet a need or help others. This kind of service is great, but simply encouraging others is often one of the best ways you can serve those around you on a daily basis. According to the apostle Paul, service and encouragement just naturally seem to go together.

Read and reflect on the following passage he wrote and then answer the questions that follow.

> For God did not appoint us to suffer wrath but to receive salvation through our Lord Jesus Christ. He died for us so that, whether we are awake or asleep, we may live together with him. Therefore encourage one another and build each other up, just as in fact you are doing.
>
> Now we ask you, brothers and sisters, to acknowledge those who work hard among you, who care for you in the Lord and who admonish you. Hold them in the highest regard in love because of their work. Live in peace with each other. And we urge you, brothers and sisters, warn those who are idle and disruptive, encourage the disheartened, help the weak, be patient with everyone. Make sure that nobody pays back wrong for wrong, but always strive to do what is good for each other and for everyone else.
>
> Rejoice always, pray continually, give thanks in all circumstances; for this is God's will for you in Christ Jesus.
>
> *1 Thessalonians 5:9–18*

How does your willingness to encourage and help others reflect on your relationship with God? What does your availability say to others about God's nature and character?

How does acknowledging the hard work of others encourage them? What does it mean to "hold them in the highest regard in love because of their work" (verse 13)?

How often do you "warn those who are idle or disruptive"? How does respectfully holding others accountable for their actions and attitudes show them the love of Jesus?

Think for a moment about the people you see on a daily basis—family, friends, neighbors, coworkers, clients or staff, the people who make your coffee or ring up your purchase. What are some ways you can encourage them in your next interactions?

REFOCUS

How would your life be different if you looked at disappointing outcomes as enticing opportunities? The truth is that God knows *exactly* what he's doing—and he is never surprised. Disappointments are often divine redirections.

Sometimes, God will block the road to motivate you to get busy and blaze a different trail.

Disappointments don't make you a victim. Rather, they prove that you are an active participant in the work that God wants to do in this world. He calls us to *participate*—not necessarily attain success or job titles or fame. So, even in the face of outcomes that you don't want, you have irrevocable agency to take the next few courageous steps. You can pivot any time you want, knowing ultimately that the affirmation and validation you may crave will only come from God—and he already approves of you!

When things don't go your way, don't scrap your entire plan. Don't get distracted! Revise it, modify it, update it, lean into it, and start enjoying it. See disappointment as a gateway to discovery and adventure on the journey. Those who live on purpose and with joy stop trying to control the outcomes. They stop thinking of life as small hops from one safe lily pad to the next. Instead, they see their lives as consisting of many great leaps of faith.

With the goal of strengthening your resolve to take risks of faith, read through Hebrews 11 in any translation of the Bible you prefer, and then answer the following questions.

How does being available to serve others require you to put faith into action? What has this looked like in your life in the past?

How do you usually feel about stepping out in faith to help others? Eager? Afraid? Bold? Something else?

Among the various giants of the faith mentioned in Hebrews 11, which one resonates with you right now? How does their story speak to your heart?

When has God surprised you by using your service to others to have an impact that exceeded your expectations? What did you learn from the experience?

RECHARGE

Jesus said a rich relationship with God is only possible by having a right relationship with each other. He said, "Whoever claims to love God yet hates a brother or sister is a liar. For whoever does not love their brother and sister, whom they have seen, cannot love God, whom they have not seen" (1 John 4:20). If we say we love God, but don't love the people he made, including the ones just as weird and insecure and fallible as we pretend not to be, then we have a heart condition we need to address. We can't keep ignoring, medicating, or being indifferent to it.

If you want to grow in your relationship with God, the fix isn't more knowledge or arguments or distractions. Serve the people around you! Don't just pursue the easy people either. Find the difficult people around you and give your heart to them in service.

So, between now and your next group session, choose someone who makes you uncomfortable—the neighbor who talks your ear off, a coworker who dresses weird, the new student from somewhere far away—and get to know that person better. Find out what you have in common. More importantly, find a way you can serve the person or meet a current need. Don't make the person a project or a way to fulfill your homework. Serve because you truly care about him or her and want to give that person a glimpse of the love of Jesus.

For Next Week: Write down any insights or questions you want to discuss at the next group meeting. In preparation for next week, read chapters 4, 11, 14, and 16 in *Undistracted.*

UNDISTRACTED IN OUR RELATIONSHIPS

By this everyone will know that you are
my disciples, if you love one another.

JOHN 13:35

WELCOME

What would happen if you told the truth about how you're *really* doing? What would it look like if someone asked, "So, how are you?"—and you responded with the honest truth? We all are conditioned to answer questions like these in ways that are less than authentic and honest. It's a common social exchange repeated millions of times on any given day.

Perhaps we do this because we feel the person asking is only being polite. Or maybe it's because we're reluctant to acknowledge we're having a not-so-good kind of day. What's more, our culture sends us the message that we are to act like we're okay all the time, regardless of how we're actually doing on the inside. After all, vulnerability is dangerous! We're supposed to have our lives together and maintain a positive attitude . . . to "fake it 'til you make it."

The sad reality is that when we sacrifice authenticity for the sake of appearances, what we're doing is basically lying. We are deceiving other people, ourselves, and perhaps even trying to lie to God about the freedom we have to be ourselves. We are denying who he made us to be and what we are actually feeling. We're withdrawing from ourselves, from others, and from the unconditional love God has for us. This is sad because God doesn't want us to try to be anything or anyone other than who we are—his masterpiece-in-the-making.

If you want to be undistracted in your relationships, you're going to have to risk telling the truth. Instead of parroting "fine" throughout your day, you're going to have say, "I'm having a tough time," or, "Work is killing me right now," or, "I'm hurting because someone I love is battling cancer." Others might be surprised at first. But they might also experience the same kind of freedom to tell *you* the truth in return. You might find that you connect with people in more meaningful ways—undistracted by what you expect one another to say.

SHARE

Take a few minutes to share any insights you have from last week's personal study. Then, to get things started, discuss one of the following questions:

- How do you usually respond when someone you know fairly well asks how you're doing? How much of the truth do you tend to share?

— *or* —

- What three words best describe how you're doing right now at this moment?

READ

Invite someone to read aloud the following passage. Listen for fresh insights as you hear the verses being read and then discuss the questions that follow.

Now a man named Ananias, together with his wife Sapphira, also sold a piece of property. With his wife's full knowledge he kept back part of the money for himself, but brought the rest and put it at the apostles' feet.

Then Peter said, "Ananias, how is it that Satan has so filled your heart that you have lied to the Holy Spirit and have kept for yourself some of the money you received for the land? Didn't it belong to you before it was sold? And after it was sold, wasn't the money at your disposal? What made you think of doing such a thing? You have not lied just to human beings but to God."

When Ananias heard this, he fell down and died. And great fear seized all who heard what had happened. Then some young men came forward, wrapped up his body, and carried him out and buried him.

About three hours later his wife came in, not knowing what had happened. Peter asked her, "Tell me, is this the price you and Ananias got for the land?"

"Yes," she said, "that is the price."

Peter said to her, "How could you conspire to test the Spirit of the Lord? Listen! The feet of the men who buried your husband are at the door, and they will carry you out also."

At that moment she fell down at his feet and died. Then the young men came in and, finding her dead, carried her out and buried her beside her husband.

Acts 5:1–10

Do you think withholding the truth about how you're feeling can compare to the deceit that Ananias and Sapphira attempted? Why or why not?

What frightens you the most in this dramatic scene in the early church? How does your fear relate to what you're going through right now in your own life?

WATCH

Play the video segment for session three (use the streaming video access provided on the inside front cover). As you watch, use the following outline to record any thoughts or concepts that stand out to you.

Sometimes when we're not authentic—when we're distracted by our appearance—we're actually lying to God. We're denying who it is that he made us to be and what it is that we're actually feeling.

Sometimes you can get distracted "running after the horse." You get off message. When this happens, go back to the "barn." **Return to your faith. Return to Jesus.**

If you get distracted and fail to connect with others, the whole idea of loving your neighbor goes out the window. You will bypass chances to meet interesting people and foster relationships.

God will use unlikely people to teach you about community. So don't get freaked out by the people that he brings into your life. Look for the opportunities around you.

Something beautiful happens when you remember how awesome it is to be spontaneous. There is certainly a good side to regimens . . . but **God's invited us into adventure** as well.

Distractions can come from our words. We're always shooting live ammo when it comes to what we say. We have to be more mindful with the words that we say.

Satan doesn't want to *destroy* you. **Satan wants to distract you.** Destroy you is one-and-done. But if he can distract you . . . that's the gift that takes forever.

If we learn to manage the distractions in our relationships, we can get back to the really important business of living our lives in a way that honors God and blesses other people.

DISCUSS

As you consider what you just watched, use the following questions to discuss these ideas, their basis in Scripture, and their application in your life with your group members.

1. Do you believe it's possible to lie to God without also attempting to lie to yourself first? Why or why not?

2. What has been the "horse" you've chased—a relationship with someone, a business deal, a certain house in a nice neighborhood, a leadership position? How has chasing it distracted you from connecting with other people in the meantime?

3. When have you risked getting to know someone different from yourself—perhaps someone you didn't think you'd like? What did you learn from relating with this person?

4. Do you tend to stick to routines and regimens, or do you enjoy being spontaneous and changing up the schedule? How does your tendency affect your ability to connect with the people you care the most about?

5. When was the last time your words—or misunderstanding of someone else's words—distracted you from getting closer to others? How was this challenge resolved?

6. What are some ways the enemy has distracted you in order to prevent you from focusing on knowing and loving others? How have you overcome these distractions?

LEARN

We all have a tendency to avoid being authentic with other people. It's so easy to get conditioned to tell them what we think they want to hear or what we think will smooth the track for a goal we're trying to reach. So, for this exercise, take a few minutes to complete the relationship inventory given below. Feel free to reconfigure the chart, but think through each category of people with whom you regularly interact and then assess your typical ways of thinking about, talking to, and acting toward them. After completing your inventory, answer the questions that follow, and then reconvene with the rest of your group.

THOUGHTS, ATTITUDES, AND INTERACTIONS I TYPICALLY HAVE WITH THESE PEOPLE:

Spouse and/or immediate family

Closest friends

Coworkers, employees, bosses

Neighbors and acquaintances

Strangers that I run into from time to time

As you look at your responses, consider which category of people surprised you the most in your assessment, and then write down what changes you will make in how you relate to them.

PRAY

Close your meeting by asking God to clear away the distractions, biases, and limiting beliefs that can prevent you from enjoying deeper relationships with others. Ask God to give each of you the courage to move beyond your comfort zone and take new risks to relate authentically with those around you. Also ask God to help you be more authentic with the people in your life.

PERSONAL STUDY

Take some time to reflect on the material you've covered this week by engaging in any or all of the following between-sessions activities. Remember, these exercises are not intended to be homework or another obligation in your busy week but are simply provided to help you process what you've been thinking and feeling since your last group time. At the start of the next session, you will have a few minutes to share any insights you learned.

REFLECT

When it comes to relationships, the Bible is pretty clear on God's guidelines for how to treat other people. The Ten Commandments and the old Levitical laws are specific about the code of conduct that God wanted his people to follow. Although Jesus fulfilled the law, it's evident that the essence of how people should treat one another remains the same.

Simply put, we are to treat others as we want to be treated, and to love our neighbors as ourselves (see Mark 12:31). Paul also explored these relationship principles in many of the letters that he wrote. Read these words he wrote to a group of believers in Ephesus and then answer the questions that follow.

> You were taught, with regard to your former way of life, to put off your old self, which is being corrupted by its deceitful desires; to be made new in the attitude of your minds; and to put on the new self, created to be like God in true righteousness and holiness.
>
> Therefore each of you must put off falsehood and speak truthfully to your neighbor, for we are all members of one body. "In your anger do not sin": Do not let the sun go down while you are still angry, and do not give the devil a foothold. Anyone who has been stealing must steal no longer, but must work, doing something useful with their own hands, that they may have something to share with those in need.
>
> Do not let any unwholesome talk come out of your mouths, but only what is helpful for building others up according to their needs, that it may benefit those who listen. And do not grieve the Holy Spirit of God, with whom you were sealed for the day of redemption. Get rid of all bitterness, rage and anger, brawling and slander, along with every form of malice. Be kind and compassionate to one another, forgiving each other, just as in Christ God forgave you.
>
> *Ephesians 4:22–32*

Look at the contrast Paul makes in the beginning of this passage. How do you treat people now as compared to the way you used to relate to others before you chose to follow Jesus?

How often does anger become a distraction in your most significant relationships? When has your anger given the devil a "foothold" to pull you away from other people?

Based on the guidelines that Paul provides, which area represents your greatest distraction when it comes to relationships? Or, to put it another way, do you struggle more with what you think about others, what you say to them, or how you act toward them?

Spend a few minutes asking God to reveal any relationships in which you need to ask forgiveness for how you've regarded (or failed to regard) particular individuals. Before going on to the next section or doing anything else, text or call anyone you need to ask for forgiveness. If possible, make a plan to meet face-to-face for this conversation.

REFOCUS

Sometimes, commitments and beliefs can limit your ability to see the bigger picture of how you are relating to others. There's a story in the Bible that tells of a time Jesus dined in the home of his close friends, Mary and Martha. One sister, Martha, was so focused on preparing a lovely meal that she missed the opportunity to just visit with him. Her intentions were sound—after all, someone had to get the food cooked and on the table—but her commitment to being a good hostess limited her availability and spontaneity. Consider how you might fall into this trap as you read the passage below and then answer the questions that follow.

> As Jesus and his disciples were on their way, he came to a village where a woman named Martha opened her home to him. She had a sister called Mary, who sat at the Lord's feet listening to what he said. But Martha was distracted by all the preparations that had to be made. She came to him and asked, "Lord, don't you care that my sister has left me to do the work by myself? Tell her to help me!"
>
> "Martha, Martha," the Lord answered, "you are worried and upset about many things, but few things are needed—or indeed only one. Mary has chosen what is better, and it will not be taken away from her."
>
> *Luke 10:38–42*

How often do you get distracted like Martha in this scene? What do you miss out on when you're overly focused on preparations and what you believe has to be done?

What does it mean for you to "sit at the feet" of someone you care about? Other than preparations, what distracts you from giving your loved ones your undivided attention?

Can you relate to Martha's anger when Mary offers no assistance to help with their meal? When have you experienced a similar situation?

What things are causing you to be worried and upset right now? How are these concerns distracting you from the few things that really matter?

RECHARGE

Review the relationship inventory exercise you completed toward the end of your last group session. Based on your assessment, who has stuck in your mind and heart the most since then? Why do you suppose you are drawn to that person right now? Does he or she have a need that you could meet, or could that person perhaps use some encouragement and support?

Before your next group session, arrange to visit with this person. Grab a coffee, eat a meal, go for a walk, window shop together . . . whatever you think you both might enjoy. Regardless of the activity, make sure you focus your attention on this person and listen to the message of his or her heart. Again, you don't want to make the person feel like a project or obligation. But let him or her know you care and want to be present.

After your visit, spend a few minutes thinking about how you can continue to let the person know that you're there for him or her. You might want to send a handwritten card or send a small gift that would make him or her smile. It could even be a text just to say you are thinking and praying about that person. However you decide to follow up, commit to making it an ongoing process of building a stronger relationship with this individual.

For Next Week: Write down any insights or questions you want to discuss at the next group meeting. In preparation for next week, read chapters 6, 9, and 12 in *Undistracted*.

UNDISTRACTED IN OUR FAITH

Fight the good fight of the faith. Take hold
of the eternal lifc to which you were called
when you made your good confession in
the presence of many witnesses.

1 TIMOTHY 6:12

WELCOME

Everyone, at times, wrestles with doubts in their faith. Faith is simple to obtain . . . but it's not always easy to live out. The author of Hebrews described faith as "confidence in what we hope for and assurance about what we do not see" (Hebrews 11:1). This kind of faith requires us to do more than just decide *who* our faith is in. It requires us to consider what our faith is actually *about*—and then have the guts to actually *do* something about what we say we believe.

Some of us bravely do this work of understanding their faith . . . while others among us ignore or defer this important work. Perhaps this is due to fear that we shouldn't ever have doubts or questions about God. But when we look at the Bible, we find that Jesus *never* had a problem with people who were uncertain in their faith. He actually chastised the people who claimed absolute certainty in an attempt to earn greater power and prestige.

So, if you've got things about your faith that you just can't get your head around, don't fake it and act like you are certain. Don't resign yourself to confusion by suppressing your thoughts and questions. Don't give in to fears that you're somehow not a good person if you have doubts. Instead, get *real* with the questions that you have. Bring them to Jesus and ask for his help in sorting them out. This will take more than a one-time prayer of introspection, but such an invitation allows God to begin the process of doing authentic work in your heart.

Don't trade what could have been a meaningful, joyful, purposeful, and fully engaged life just so you can fit in, be accepted, or feel like you are part of the crew. If your faith is important to you, then you have to decide what you really believe . . . and leave behind the distractions of assumptions, mistruths, and human-fueled systems. As you do, remember that God loves you and accepts you as you are. In fact, one of the enduring treasures of the message that Jesus came in person to deliver is summarized in two simple words: *you belong.*

SHARE

Take a few minutes to share any insights you have from last week's personal study. Then, to get things started, discuss one of the following questions:

- How do you respond to the idea that it's okay to have doubts in your faith?

— *or* —

- Where do you experience closeness with God most consistently?

READ

Invite someone to read aloud the following passage. Listen for fresh insights as you hear the verses being read and then discuss the questions that follow.

Immediately Jesus made the disciples get into the boat and go on ahead of him to the other side, while he dismissed the crowd. After he had dismissed them, he went up on a mountainside by himself to pray. Later that night, he was there alone, and the boat was already a considerable distance from land, buffeted by the waves because the wind was against it.

Shortly before dawn Jesus went out to them, walking on the lake. When the disciples saw him walking on the lake, they were terrified. "It's a ghost," they said, and cried out in fear.

But Jesus immediately said to them: "Take courage! It is I. Don't be afraid."

"Lord, if it's you," Peter replied, "tell me to come to you on the water."

"Come," he said.

Then Peter got down out of the boat, walked on the water and came toward Jesus. But when he saw the wind, he was afraid and, beginning to sink, cried out, "Lord, save me!"

Immediately Jesus reached out his hand and caught him. "You of little faith," he said, "why did you doubt?"

And when they climbed into the boat, the wind died down. Then those who were in the boat worshiped him, saying, "Truly you are the Son of God."

Matthew 14:22–33

What do you think distracted the disciples and kept them from recognizing Jesus walking on the water? The storm? Their own fears? Something else?

What is required for us to take courage and trust the presence of Jesus in our lives? How do distractions undermine our courage and fracture our faith?

WATCH

Play the video segment for session four (use the streaming video access provided on the inside front cover). As you watch, use the following outline to record any thoughts or concepts that stand out to you.

When we get distracted in our faith, the first thing to sink is **our ability to connect with Jesus**. Like Peter, we start seeing the storm and the water around us and no longer see Christ.

Jesus wants to walk back to the boat with you. There is no shame in losing contact with him. There is just the distraction that took you away. Eliminate the distraction and **get back in the boat with Jesus**.

Find someone safe with whom you can discuss your questions about faith. **Find someone who knows the Scriptures** . . . or at least find somebody who *wants* to jump into the Scriptures with you.

Don't freak out when something unlikely happens. There will be times when you, like Peter, feel like you're going down. In those moments, Jesus will be there to grab you wrist-to-wrist.

Get into the habit of checking things against Scripture. If what you are think-ing squares with Scripture, share it with others. But if it doesn't square with Scripture, don't pass it along.

You don't have to maintain the appearance of looking like you've got it all together. Just **get real with somebody** and say, "I'm in desperate need for answers that only God can give me."

There is something freeing about admitting to some of the things that have tripped you up in your life. After all, **you cannot live in the future with a foot stuck in the past**.

What is it that is distracting us in our faith? What is it that we are running away from? We need to **see it, so we can understand it, so Jesus can fix it**.

DISCUSS

As you consider what you just watched, use the following questions to discuss these ideas, their basis in Scripture, and their application in your life with your group members.

1. What are the greatest distractions to growing in your faith right now? How have you tried to overcome them?

2. When were times that you were "walking on water" in your relationship with Jesus but then got distracted? What impact did being distracted have on your spiritual growth?

3. How have you experienced the extended hand of Jesus when distracted in your faith? How have you reconnected with him after distractions have pulled you away?

4. When struggling in your faith, what are some of the doubts and questions with which you often wrestle? How have you handled these challenges in the past?

5. What are some effective ways that you have found to connect with God each day?

6. How has growing in your faith made you more comfortable in being who God made you to be? What impact has this awareness had in other areas of your life?

LEARN

Even when we're consistently spending time with God, we may still struggle in our faith. Nagging questions can persist and pull us away from the trust we long to have in our relationship with God. Or we may experience personal losses or trials that leave us feeling shaken in our trust in a loving God. Although the Bible tells us that God's ways are above our ways (see Isaiah 55:8), we're nonetheless left feeling confused, uncertain, and conflicted.

It's okay to have these feelings, thoughts, and questions. Surely, the disciple Peter must have been shaken when he realized that he was sinking into the stormy sea! But the key to being undistracted by them is to *take them to Jesus*.

We allow him to reach down, grab us "wrist to wrist," and lift us above the stormy waters of danger and fears.

As you consider this, pair up with someone you haven't previously connected with in the group. Take turns spending a few minutes sharing one question, challenge, or concern that sometimes causes you to struggle in your faith. Listen carefully to each another and don't try to solve or resolve whatever your respective struggles may be. Finish by praying for one another regarding these matters before reconvening with the rest of your group.

PRAY

Wrap up this session by sharing any requests you would like the group to lift up in prayer, including any related to the exercises you just completed. Thank God for the ways that he has reached out to you in the past when your faith has started slipping. Ask him for peace and power to help those who may be struggling right now. Finally, praise him for the ways he provides security, stability, and strength no matter what questions or doubts you may have.

PERSONAL STUDY

Take some time to reflect on the material you've covered this week by engaging in any or all of the following between-sessions activities. Remember, these exercises are not intended to be homework or another obligation in your busy week but are simply provided to help you process what you've been thinking and feeling since your last group time. At the start of the next session, you will have a few minutes to share any insights you learned.

REFLECT

Distractions can emerge in your faith when your *beliefs* and *behaviors* are not aligned. You should bring your doubts and questions to God, but you should also keep doing what you know God wants you to do, especially when it comes to loving and serving others. In the Bible, we read of an encounter that Jesus had with a young man who had questions about his faith. This man seems to have believed the *truth* of God's Word and Jesus' teaching, but ultimately he could not follow through and *act* on what God's Word was telling him to do. Read through this story carefully and then answer the questions that follow.

> As Jesus started on his way, a man ran up to him and fell on his knees before him. "Good teacher," he asked, "what must I do to inherit eternal life?"
>
> "Why do you call me good?" Jesus answered. "No one is good—except God alone. You know the commandments: 'You shall not murder, you shall not commit adultery, you shall not steal, you shall not give false testimony, you shall not defraud, honor your father and mother.'"
>
> "Teacher," he declared, "all these I have kept since I was a boy."
>
> Jesus looked at him and loved him. "One thing you lack," he said. "Go, sell everything you have and give to the poor, and you will have treasure in heaven. Then come, follow me."
>
> At this the man's face fell. He went away sad, because he had great wealth.
>
> *Mark 10:17–22*

Based on this man's words and actions, what might his motive have been in asking Jesus this particular question? Do you believe this man already knew the answer that Jesus gave him?

What might have been Jesus' intention in asking, "Why do you call me good?" Why do you think he then added, "No one is good—except God alone"?

What is the one thing this man lacked based on what Jesus instructed him to do? How would doing as Jesus instructed provide this "one thing"?

What prevented this man from following through and doing as Jesus instructed? What was the source of this man's sadness?

REFOCUS

Many of us today are guilty of "stalking" Jesus. We have memorized Bible verses and know lots of things about him. We have read stories of him loving and serving others. We admire him from afar. But we haven't taken him up on his offer to get to know him personally.

Jesus once said to the crowds that followed him, "Not everyone who says to me, 'Lord, Lord,' will enter the kingdom of heaven, but only the one who does the will of my Father who is in heaven" (Matthew 7:21). It's good to study the Bible and expound on theology . . . but we have to *act* on what we believe. It's good to know what God says about helping the poor and the widows and the orphans . . but we have to then do something practical to help them. It's good to give of our money and resources . . . but we have to also give of ourselves.

Remember that Jesus told the rich young man in the previous story to sell his possessions and then follow him. Both actions were required for him to remove the distractions and focus singularly and intentionally on knowing God and showing his love to others. Likewise, we need to be following the example of Jesus through our actions. With this goal in mind, read the following words that Jesus told his followers and then answer the questions below.

"Do not store up for yourselves treasures on earth, where moths and vermin destroy, and where thieves break in and steal. But store up for yourselves treasures in heaven, where moths and vermin do not destroy, and where thieves do not break in and steal. For where your treasure is, there your heart will be also.

"The eye is the lamp of the body. If your eyes are healthy, your whole body will be full of light. But if your eyes are unhealthy, your whole body will be full of darkness. If then the light within you is darkness, how great is that darkness!

"No one can serve two masters. Either you will hate the one and love the other, or you will be devoted to the one and despise the other. You cannot serve both God and money."

Matthew 6:19–24

Looking honestly at the patterns in your life, where have you ever been guilty of "stalking" Jesus? How does your knowledge of him compare to your actual relationship with him?

Do you agree that "where your treasure is, there your heart will be also"? Why or why not?

While "treasures on earth" refers to money in Christ's warning, your treasure can also manifest itself in other ways—such as homes, cars, possessions, status symbols, achievements, fame, and on and on. What kind of treasure is distracting you the most right now?

Jesus' comment that the "eye is the lamp of the body" is a reminder that we need to keep our focus fixed on him. What happens when your eyes are "healthy"? How does keeping your eyes fixed on Christ enable you to see past the darkness of distractions?

RECHARGE

You may be familiar with the concept of having a "quiet time" with God each day. This is generally a designated appointment with God—often first thing in the morning—when you study the Bible and pray. Perhaps this works for you, which is great. But for many people, quiet times become just another item on their daily checklist . . . an obligation to help them feel they have "measured up" and can consider themselves good Christians.

Quiet times are never specifically mentioned in the Bible in the way that we often think of them. Yes, Jesus would get up "very early in the morning" to pray (Mark 1:35). But he also prayed in the afternoon and evening (see Matthew 14:22–23) and at night (see Luke 6:12). The reality is that God doesn't care whether you have what has tradition-ally been known as a "quiet time." He just wants you to connect with him, be aware of his presence continually, and be available when he calls you to act and serve. Being intentional is good . . . but how you focus your attention on God without distractions is what matters most.

If early morning is your best time to read the Bible and reflect on God . . . then terrific. If not, find another time. Whenever you do it, feel free to make it as loud, quiet, active, or meditative as you need it to be to propel you forward in your faith. If the traditions, structures, and practices that your faith community came up with don't help you surround your life with Jesus, scrap them and come up with something newer and better for you.

Before your next group session, experiment with at least a couple of different ways to focus your mind and heart on God. Volunteer at a food bank or shelter. Help out with the music program at church. Practice your music skills or take up woodworking. Take a walk in nature and express your appreciation to God. He would rather have you fully engaged with him while swimming laps or mentoring kids than to have you sitting quietly like you're in detention each day. So find something that works for you. When it stops working, find something new.

For Next Week: Write down any insights or questions you want to discuss at the next group meeting. In preparation for next week, read chapters 1, 2, and 17 in *Undistracted.*

UNDISTRACTED IN OUR PURPOSE

The purposes of a person's heart are deep waters,

but one who has insight draws them out.

PROVERBS 20:5

WELCOME

Sometimes we can make living out our purpose overly complicated. We question if we have accurately identified what we should be doing. We wonder if we are taking the right steps to get there. We worry that we are moving too fast or too slow. But God has already given us an all-access pass to exercise our unique purpose. We just need to show up and claim it.

Of course, using your all-access pass will take a good dose of boldness. If you want the freedom to go anywhere and do what God has uniquely created and equipped you to do . . . a mindset shift has to take place. You will have to get *undistracted*. This means taking the steps that you believe God is calling *you* to take. It means knocking down the fears that everyone else is the gatekeeper of your life. It means getting rid of the notion that you have to ask others for permission to live into what God has already placed in your heart. Simply put, it means living like you have already been invited into the beautiful life that God has for you instead of wondering if you are where you really belong or have the right to be there.

Now is the time to ask yourself why you keep heading for the predictability and obscurity of the "rafters," where you can only look on from afar, rather than moving a little closer to the "stage" where the action takes place. Sure, you can play it safe and head for the faraway places. The Bible says that even the disciples looked on from afar at times. Or you can take God up on his invitation to a much less predictable path filled with an eclectic and diverse assortment of people who are also living out their faith in the "mosh pit."

Figuring out where your unique ticket allows you to go will require you to ask what it is that you really want to do with your life. It will then require you to summon the grit you'll need to move past distractions that take your focus off reaching that goal. For the truth is that you *will* face barriers, naysayers, pressures, injustices, the misguided advice of others, and other obstacles that will seek to obscure your view. An all-access pass isn't a cheat code for living an easy life. But it is the key to experiencing a more purposeful and joyful one.

SHARE

Take a few minutes to share any insights you have from last week's personal study. Then, to get things started, discuss one of the following questions:

- Since beginning this study, what has changed in how you view distractions in your life? How much progress have you made in overcoming distractions?

— *or* —

- Considering all you've learned so far, how would you complete this statement" "Going forward, I most want to focus on being undistracted in my _____ (attitude, service, relationships, faith, purpose)."

READ

Invite someone to read aloud the following passage. Listen for fresh insights as you hear the verses being read and then discuss the questions that follow.

"When the Son of Man comes in his glory, and all the angels with him, he will sit on his glorious throne. All the nations will be gathered before him, and he will separate the people one from another as a shepherd separates the sheep from the goats. He will put the sheep on his right and the goats on his left.

"Then the King will say to those on his right, 'Come, you who are blessed by my Father; take your inheritance, the kingdom prepared for you since the creation of the world. For I was hungry and you gave me something to eat, I was thirsty and you gave me something to drink, I was a stranger and you invited me in, I needed clothes and you clothed me, I was sick and you looked after me, I was in prison and you came to visit me.'

"Then the righteous will answer him, 'Lord, when did we see you hungry and feed you, or thirsty and give you something to drink? When did we see you a stranger and invite you in, or needing clothes and clothe you? When did we see you sick or in prison and go to visit you?'

"The King will reply, 'Truly I tell you, whatever you did for one of the least of these brothers and sisters of mine, you did for me.'"

Matthew 25:31-40

When you consider all the criteria Jesus could have mentioned as to those who will be considered "blessed," why do you think he chose to cite meeting basic human needs?

Jesus identifies service to him with service to "the least of these brothers and sisters"? How does serving the tangible needs of other people—for food and drink, clothing and shelter, hospitality and comfort—serve Christ and advance his purposes in this world?

WATCH

Play the video segment for session five (use the streaming video access provided on the inside front cover). As you watch, use the following outline to record any thoughts or concepts that stand out to you.

Waypoints provide smaller targets for reaching larger goals. They help you stay undistracted in your purpose. You stop *drifting* aimlessly in life and start *heading* toward a destination.

Identifying your purpose can be challenging. But remember that Jesus identified his purpose as helping those in need—hungry people, thirsty people, sick people, strange people, naked people, people in jail (see Matthew 25:35–36). James also mentions taking care of widows and orphans (see James 1:27).

Consider your purpose like a jigsaw puzzle. First find the four corners, and then find the edge pieces. Focus on discovering your purpose one piece at a time.

If you're going to get reconnected with your purpose, you need to get your head on a swivel and **realize Jesus is already in the room**. Assume he is right there with you and be situationally aware.

When it comes to finding your undistracted purpose, **you have an all-access pass.** Quit waiting for other people's permission or a group consensus on what you should be doing. Instead, look to the Scriptures and focus on what God has already given permission for you to do.

The apostle Paul encourages us to **take a genuine interest in others** (see Philippians 2:20). Take a deeper dive and say, "Who are you? How did you come to be you? What does it feel like to be you?"

If God himself tells you not to do something . . . then for Pete's sake, don't do it. But otherwise, get after your beautiful dream. **Go after that ambition.** Throw everything you've got at it.

Get less distracted by people's approval and more distracted by God's approval. Set a couple of waypoints to guide you along the way. You will make progress and move toward the feet of Jesus.

DISCUSS

As you consider what you just watched, use the following questions to discuss these ideas, their basis in Scripture, and their application in your life with your group members.

1. What waypoint have you recently reached toward fulfilling a larger goal? What waypoints do you still need to set to fulfill that goal?

2. How does meeting the physical needs of others factor into the way you live out your purpose? How does your purpose practically serve those around you?

3. If you consider your purpose to be a kind of jigsaw puzzle, how much of it do you have filled in? What image is coming into view to help you clarify what you're made to do?

4. When have you waited for permission before taking the next step to do what God has already called you to do? How do you handle this tendency to seek permission now?

5. What are some ways you show genuine concern for the welfare of others? What are you presently doing to practice your purpose in serving others?

6. How have you overcome the distraction of critics and naysayers and continued doing what you know God wants you to do? What advice would you tell other believers about how to handle the resistance they may receive in living out their purpose?

LEARN

As this study wraps up, remember to continue supporting those in your group as you seek to eliminate distractions, focus on living out your God-given purpose, and deepen your relationship with the Lord. Throughout the sessions, emphasis has been placed on putting truth and faith into *action* rather than just *thinking* or *talking* about these things. Serving others clearly emerges as a way to reflect the love of God and obey the teachings of Christ. So what better way to conclude your group time than by coming up with a commencement exercise!

Spend a few minutes brainstorming needs and causes in your local community that your entire group could come together to serve. It might be through your church, but it might also be simply an individual need a group member has observed in their neighborhood—for example, mowing the lawn or doing basic maintenance for someone unable to do so.

Don't spend too long brainstorming these ideas, because there are tons of great causes and plenty of people in need. Just settle on one as the majority of the group feels led and make a plan for how you can take action to help in the week to come. Remember, this doesn't have to be a big deal . . . like a fundraiser or food drive. It should just be a way to practice what you've all been learning and processing during these past five sessions. Write down what the group decides to do below as well as next steps on how to implement the plan.

Need, goal, or cause our group will help:

Ways we will help these people:

Next steps in carrying out our plan:

Deadline for the group to complete this goal:

PRAY

Conclude this final session by going around the group and sharing one thing you are especially thankful for, one personal need you want lifted up, and one hope for the group based on what you've learned. Thank God for how you've been challenged and inspired by all you have learned. Ask God for protection from the enemy and the distractions he will send your way as you implement what you've learned. Pray for wisdom and discernment to become more undistracted in your life and more fully engaged with the needs of those around you.

PERSONAL STUDY

Take some time to reflect on the material you've covered this final week by engaging in any or all of the following between-sessions activities. Remember, these exercises are not intended to be homework or another obligation in your busy week but are provided to help you process what you've been thinking and feeling since your last group time. In this final time of reflection, you may also want to review your previous answers, either going back to previous personal studies in this guide or referring to the journal or notebook you used for your responses. In the coming days, be sure to share any insights you learned with one of your fellow group members.

REFLECT

Take a moment today to praise God for all that you've learned and experienced over the past few weeks. Once again, the book of Psalms in the Bible offers many wonderful ways to begin a time of thanksgiving for what God has done. So, with this mind, read the passage below (or find another favorite psalm of your choosing) and offer your gratitude for how God is helping you become more undistracted. Use the questions that follow to aid in your reflection.

It is good to praise the LORD
   and make music to your name, O Most High,
proclaiming your love in the morning
   and your faithfulness at night,
to the music of the ten-stringed lyre
   and the melody of the harp.
For you make me glad by your deeds, LORD;
   I sing for joy at what your hands have done.
How great are your works, LORD,
   how profound your thoughts!
Senseless people do not know,
   fools do not understand,
that though the wicked spring up like grass
   and all evildoers flourish,
   they will be destroyed forever.
But you, LORD, are forever exalted.
For surely your enemies, LORD,
   surely your enemies will perish;
   all evildoers will be scattered.
You have exalted my horn like that of a wild ox;
   fine oils have been poured on me.
My eyes have seen the defeat of my adversaries;
   my ears have heard the rout of my wicked foes.

The righteous will flourish like a palm tree,
    they will grow like a cedar of Lebanon;
planted in the house of the LORD,
    they will flourish in the courts of our God.
They will still bear fruit in old age,
    they will stay fresh and green,
proclaiming, "The LORD is upright;
    he is my Rock, and there is no wickedness
    in him."

Psalm 92:1–15

What are the benefits of thanking God for all the blessings you're experiencing right now? How does gratitude help overcome distractions and focus your attention on your true priorities?

For whom or what are you especially thankful to God right now? Why?

What aspects of God's character mean the most to you as you conclude this group experience? What have you learned about who God is that will affect how you relate to him going forward?

What are some of the specific things from meeting with your group, reading the *Undistracted* book, or completing this study that have had the greatest impact on you? (Focus on what you're especially grateful to have experienced and learned throughout this process.)

REFOCUS

Flip back through your notes, questions, and reflections that you've written down, both during your group meetings and also your between-session personal studies. Look at your GUMPS list from session one and your relationship inventory exercise from session three. Then answer the following questions as you evaluate your overall experience and its impact on you.

As you go through your notes and reflections, what stands out the most to you? Are there consistent themes or threads you see running throughout the five sessions?

How has your relationship with God changed over the course of meeting with your group? Where do you see evidence of this change in notes and written reflections? In your actions?

How has your focus become more undistracted since you started this study? What have you learned about how to focus on your priorities that wasn't clear to you before?

What passage or verses from the Bible have empowered you the most as you seek to overcome distractions and focus on deepening your faith and living out your unique purpose? Why do you think this truth from the Bible means so much to you?

RECHARGE

Spend a few final moments bringing each group member to mind and considering how they contributed to your overall experience during the study. Use the following questions to help you bring closure to this time, even as you carry your experience with you and continue to follow Jesus and enjoy the amazing adventure of faith you're living each day.

What are some of the moments that stand out to you the most during this study? How have others in the group helped you to get *undistracted* as you pursue your purpose?

What surprised you the most during this study? What disappointed you?

What will you carry with you now that your group has concluded this study? How have you changed since starting and completing these sessions?

Fill in the blank: "After this study, what I'll remember most is _____ ."

Before more than a week has passed after your last meeting, choose at least one other group member and send him or her a text, email, or call to see how things are going. When you connect with the person, ask who he or she chose to reach out to from your group. Try to make sure that *everyone* in your group hears from someone else. Finally, if the group wants to continue meeting, make a plan for your next study. Or, if the group disbands, continue checking on the friends you've made and asking how you can pray for them.

LEADER'S GUIDE

Thank you for your willingness to lead a small group through this study. What you have chosen to do is valuable and will make a great difference in the lives of others. The rewards of being a leader are different from those of participating, and we hope that as you lead you will find your own journey with Jesus deepened by the experience.

Undistracted is a five-session Bible study built around video content and small-group interaction. As the group leader, imagine yourself as the host of a party. Your job is to take care of your guests by managing the behind-the-scenes details so that as your guests arrive, they can focus on one another and on the interaction around the topic for that week.

Your role as the group leader is not to answer all the questions or reteach the content— the video, book, and study guide will do most of that work. Your job is to guide the experience and cultivate your small group into a connected and engaged community. This will make it a place for members to process, question, and reflect—not necessarily receive more instruction.

There are several elements in this leader's guide that will help you as you structure your study and reflection time, so be sure to follow along and take advantage of each one.

BEFORE YOU BEGIN

Before your first meeting, make sure the members have a copy of this study guide. Alternately, you can hand out the study guides at your first meeting and give the members some time to look over the material and ask any preliminary questions. Also make sure they are aware they have access to the videos at any time through the streaming code provided on the inside front cover. During your first meeting, send a sheet of paper around the room and have the members write down their name, phone number, and email address so you can keep in touch.

Generally, the ideal size for a group is eight to ten people, which will ensure everyone has time to participate in discussions. If you have more people, you might want to break up the main group into smaller subgroups. Encourage those who show up at the first meeting to commit to attending the duration of the study, as this will help the group members get to know one another, create stability for the group, and help you know how to best prepare each week.

Each of the sessions begins with an opening reflection. The questions that follow in the "Share" section serve as an icebreaker to get the group members thinking about the general topic at hand. Some people may want to tell a long story in response to one of these questions, but the goal is to keep the answers brief. Ideally, you want everyone in the group to get a chance to answer, so try to keep the responses to a minute or less. If you have talkative group members, say up front that everyone needs to limit their answer to one minute.

Give the group members a chance to answer, but also tell them to feel free to pass if they wish. With the rest of the study, it's generally not a good idea to have everyone answer every question—a free-flowing discussion is more desirable. But with the opening icebreaker questions, you can go around the circle. Encourage shy people to share, but don't force them.

At your first meeting, let the group members know each session contains a personal study section that they can use to reflect more on the content during the week. While this is an optional exercise, it will help the members cement the concepts presented during the group study time and encourage them to spend time each day in the Bible. Let them know that if they choose to do so, they can watch the video for the following week by accessing the streaming code found on the inside front cover of their studies. Invite them to bring any questions and insights they uncovered to your next meeting, especially if they didn't understand something.

WEEKLY PREPARATION

As the leader, there are a few things you should do to prepare for each meeting:

- *Read through the session.* This will help you to become more familiar with the content and know how to structure the discussion times.

- *Decide how the videos will be used.* Determine whether you want the members to watch the videos ahead of time (via the streaming access code found on the inside front cover) or together as a group.
- *Decide which questions you want to discuss.* Based on the amount and length of group discussion, you may not be able to get through all the questions, so choose four to five that you definitely want to cover.
- *Be familiar with the questions you want to discuss.* When the group meets, you'll be watching the clock, so you want to make sure you are familiar with the questions you have selected. In this way, you'll ensure you have the material more deeply in your mind than your group members.
- *Pray for your group.* Pray for your group members throughout the week and ask God to lead them as they study his Word.

In many cases, there will be no one "right" answer to the question. Answers will vary, especially when the group members are being asked to share their personal experiences.

STRUCTURING THE DISCUSSION TIME

You will need to determine with your group how long you want to meet each week so you can plan your time accordingly. Generally, most groups like to meet for either ninety minutes or two hours, so you could use one of the following schedules:

SECTION	90 MINUTES	120 MINUTES
Welcome (members arrive and get settled)	10 minutes	15 minutes
Share (discuss one or more of the opening questions for the session)	10 minutes	15 minutes
Read (discuss the questions based on the Scripture reading for the week)	10 minutes	15 minutes
Watch (watch the teaching material together and take notes)	15 minutes	15 minutes
Discuss (discuss the Bible study questions you selected ahead of time)	25 minutes	35 minutes
Learn (go through the closing exercise)	10 minutes	15 minutes
Pray (pray together as a group and dismiss)	10 minutes	10 minutes

As the group leader, it is up to you to keep track of the time and keep things on schedule. You might want to set a timer for each segment so both you and the group members know when your time is up. (There are some good phone apps for timers that play a gentle chime or other pleasant sound instead of a disruptive noise.)

Don't be concerned if the group members are quiet or slow to share. People are often quiet when they are pulling together their ideas, and this might be a new experience for them. Just ask a question and let it hang in the air until someone shares. You can then say, "Thank you. What about others? What came to you when you watched that portion of the teaching?"

GROUP DYNAMICS

Leading a group through *Undistracted* will prove to be highly rewarding both to you and your group members. But you still may encounter challenges along the way! Discussions can get off track. Group members may not be sensitive to the needs and ideas of others. Some might worry they will be expected to talk about matters that make them feel awkward. Others may express comments that result in disagreements. To help ease this strain on you and the group, consider the following ground rules:

- When someone raises a question or comment that is off the main topic, suggest that you deal with it another time, or, if you feel led to go in that direction, let the group know you will be spending some time discussing it.
- If someone asks a question that you don't know how to answer, admit it and move on. At your discretion, feel free to invite group members to comment on questions that call for personal experience.
- If you find one or two people are dominating the discussion time, direct a few questions to others in the group. Outside the main group time, ask the more dominating members to help you draw out the quieter ones. Work to make them a part of the solution instead of part of the problem.
- When a disagreement occurs, encourage the group members to process the matter in love. Encourage those on opposite sides to restate what they heard the

other side say about the matter, and then invite each side to evaluate if that perception is accurate. Lead the group in examining other Scriptures related to the topic and look for common ground.

When any of these issues arise, encourage your group members to follow these words from the Bible: "Love one another" (John 13:34), "If it is possible, as far as it depends on you, live at peace with everyone" (Romans 12:18), "Whatever is true . . . noble . . . right . . . if anything is excellent or praiseworthy—think about such things" (Philippians 4:8), and "Be quick to listen, slow to speak and slow to become angry" (James 1:19). This will make your group time more rewarding and beneficial for everyone who attends.

Thank you again for taking the time to lead your group. You are making a difference in the lives of others and having an impact on helping others get *undistracted*.

COMPANION BOOK TO ENRICH YOUR STUDY EXPERIENCE

Available wherever books are sold

New Video Study for Your Church or Small Group

If you've enjoyed this book, now you can go deeper with the companion video Bible study!

In this five-session study, Bob Goff helps you apply the principles in *Dream Big* to your life. The study guide includes video notes, group discussion questions, and personal study and reflection materials for in-between sessions.

Available now at your favorite bookstore, or streaming video on StudyGateway.com.

THOMAS NELSON
® *Since 1798*

ALSO AVAILABLE FROM BOB GOFF

Driven by Bob's trademark storytelling, *Everybody, Always* reveals the lessons Bob learned–often the hard way–about what it means to love without inhibition, insecurity, or restriction. From finding the right friends to discovering the upside of failure, *Everybody Always* points the way to embodying love by doing the unexpected, the intimidating, the seemingly impossible.

Video Bible Study Also Available

| Streaming
Video | Book
9780718078133 | DVD
9780310095361 | Study Guide
9780310095330 |